"*Red Obsidian* is bold, clean, as i   ıg:
luminous and its own element, yₑ   er,
ancient place. Torre writes in the v   ᵤᵤ, Merwin and
Heaney. Like them, he lives in a wₑ ₔₔ ᵣarely accessible: yet here it is,
magically durable, and losing none of its luster in the transference. He's
one of North America's greatest living poets." —RICK BASS, author of
For a Little While

"*Red Obsidian* is a book for the ages. Full of grit and wonder, grief and
exhilaration, these poems throw off sparks. What a stunning testament
to a world worked over, silted up, yet full of wings." — KATE HARRIS,
author of *Lands of Lost Borders*

"From the fierce joy and naming of wilderness labour, to the deep stillness
of its contemplation, these poems light up the mind and the heart."
—DORIANNE LAUX, author of *Only as the Day Is Long*

"By turns litany and chant, lyric and dirge—an intense and empathetic
voice." —ALICE MAJOR, author of *Welcome to the Anthropocene*

"Like a prize-fighter boxing over his weight, Stephan Torre has long made
his home in the wilderness, negotiating environments that are the hostile,
inhospitable, and often dangerous—places where a neighbour might ask
without irony, 'don't ya wanna stay here / and fight the elements?' Torre's
poems inhabit the same liminal space, straddling the domesticated and
the untamed, the raw and the despoiled. The wilderness Torre describes
is not pastoral; forests and wildlife coexist with tractors, chainsaws, and
gutted animals. Your place there is earned. The poems in *Red Obsidian*
channel a chorus of ancient Chinese poets…to praise our wounded
but unyielding world. Stephan Torres's poems are lyrical, muscular,
unflinching, and necessary." —GARY YOUNG, author of *That's What I
Thought and Even So*

ᎠꭲbᎧ

OSKANA POETRY & POETICS

Stephan Torre

Red Obsidian

University of Regina Press

Printed and bound in Canada at Imprimerie Gauvin. The text of this book is printed on 100% post-consumer recycled paper with earth-friendly vegetable-based inks.

Cover art: Duncan Noel Campbell

Cover and text design: Duncan Campbell, University of Regina Press

Editor: Randy Lundy
Proofreader: Donna Grant

The text and titling faces are Arno, designed by Robert Slimbach.

Library and Archives Canada Cataloguing in Publication

Title: Red obsidian / Stephan Torre.

Other titles: Poems. Selections

Names: Torre, Stephan, author.

Series: Oskana poetry & poetics.

Description: Series statement: Oskana poetry and poetics | "New and selected poems"—Cover.

Identifiers: Canadiana (print) 20200358421 | Canadiana (ebook) 20200358588 | ISBN 9780889777750 (softcover) | ISBN 9780889777774 (PDF) | ISBN 9780889777798 (EPUB)

Classification: LCC PS8639.O77 A6 2021 | DDC C811/.6—DC23

10 9 8 7 6 5 4 3 2 1

UNIVERSITY OF REGINA PRESS
University of Regina
Regina, Saskatchewan
Canada S4S 0A2
TELEPHONE: (306) 585-4758
FAX: (306) 585-4699
WEB: www.uofrpress.ca
EMAIL: uofrpress@uregina.ca

We acknowledge the support of the Canada Council for the Arts for our publishing program. We acknowledge the financial support of the Government of Canada. / Nous reconnaissons l'appui financier du gouvernement du Canada. This publication was made possible with support from Creative Saskatchewan's Book Publishing Production Grant Program.

for Judy (mi pilota)

... to live if it would let them.
They went as far as they could.
The lucky ones with their shadows.
—W.S. MERWIN

... When the poem
Contest is ended, someone
Sings a song of the South. And
I think of my little boat,
And long to be on my way.
—TU FU

CONTENTS

Crowberries: *New Poems*

IV

from
Man Living on a Side Creek

I remember how we balanced on the springboard
with our axes, how the chips soared
past Boonville and San Francisco.
I remember the song of the misery whip,
the taste of good steel, how our shoulders
soaked the sawdust.
The clear acid of those mornings
cut through my body
with the blood of alders and suckers,
the osprey's salty claw.

I remember dogging the endless chain, yelling
at the mules, deep ruts through the ferns,
smoke and groaning oxen.
I was coiling rope and cranking the log jack
as they crushed hillsides rolling into the river.
I remember farmers who spent their whole lives
feeding smouldering stumps, their sheep
biting red clay.

I stoked the steam donkey, leaping with sparks
as the huge winch cable tightened on the drum,
gutting the darkness. I danced
on the mill pond like Ahab
(a banana slug clinging to my boot).
I remember the grunting
as we canted the shaggy giants off the skidway
and drove in the dogs, dog teeth in my liver
as we tore into the purple old growth: the Sinker,
the Blue One... head saw singing,
thunder of the carriage, slabs of gigantic meat,

our eyes all bloodshot with happiness,
the glowing mountain of bone meal
against the blue sea—
salt lips of a motherless morning.

Cool odour of crushed fruit, sawdust
like a blast of wheat
through my ribs.
I remember the pit of silence
when the smokestack guttered, the flat belts
and rollers whined still, and I saw the sun
standing in a pool of ravens.

I remember the stain on the brakeman's suspenders,
the harness of the white gelding
on the loading dock, the beautiful slime
of the pilings, the small wrists of the mill-owner's wife.
I remember the schooner ploughing in
through unbelievable rocks and foam,
the red grin of the captain.

Up the canyon, when we dropped
to rest, we could hear the sea breaking,
sometimes a rush of doves.
We were splitting open old buckskin
logs, redwood butts and punkins
hand loggers left by the creek
when they went for more booze,
long before a saw log got winched out of here.
We never heard the dolphins
strangling in the drag nets, we couldn't see
the stain spreading out from the stern,
the horizon turning brown.

Our paths cut down through Costanoan midden,
abalone shell, lupine and granite dust.
We broke an urchin open
on the slippery rock, squeezed a lemon
and sucked the sharp morning from our hands.
On a minus tide it was all there to dig
and pry from the hissing cliff, one swell after
another, before the big plate glass was tilted up
around brass fittings, before the coast
road was oiled slick as another roll of film
and tanker diesels churned the milkshake yellow.

We pumped south of Malpaso Creek for rock fish
or some bawdy wisdom before Hollywood
came and cut the old ranches up
for props. Beyond the little boat
pulling in snapper and cabazone
a barge line was stretching tight
to Japan, but we didn't see it.

Light shattered in the kelp
between our laughter and the big slick
blubber flukes rolling south
out of sight. The blown ridges plunged down
into mist, and the headlands, long and ragged
as a condor's wing, kept curving
out of sight.

We thought the seams of the freighters were welded
tight as we climbed up through coyote bush
to raise our kids in a blaze of redtails.
We believed we could hoist and chink the stones
Jeffers left grinding below the scenic ocean
drive, thought the trails to our rustic towers
would be too rough for the inspectors, too steep
for the realtors. We couldn't see
the factory ships flushing their bilges,
the old-growth forest piled high
on the barge decks, north creeks running red
mud out of clearcuts and smoking craters,
our dream coast hacked and hauled off for sushi
while folk music played
in our cabins, and we believed
our muddy roads would keep out the world.

HEADLAND FARM

The tractor rusts by a lizard
in foggy thistles.

Horse harness rots off its spike
in the windy shed.

Cattle scratch their lice under the eaves
until the grey house collapses.

A hawk chops out of the mist.

What did they want
of this red clay, seacoast
bulging with birds and deep grass?

His back to the sun, he drove pickets
down to the edge of the headland.
His face burned like plough steel,
and morning smoked in his footsteps.

What did they want, turning the meadow
over and over, until the barn filled
with ocean, and the moon sank
in the cellar?

Berries blackened at the sill.
Her face tightened against the wind, her voice
blew out like chaff.

Season by season they became
strangers to the sea
and to each other.

A man pushes himself
until the land warps
like the boards he loved.

Pushes until bitterness has carved his hand
into a root that holds
a rusty cup, and he has forgotten
that he was thirsty, or in love.

I remember that camp,
coyotes rooting sagebrush,
mesas of dry blood,
the scorpion beside our fire.

You knew as well
as I, the ghosts
of cactus and lava
wanted to sleep.

The arroyos were full
of tragic sand, bones
ground by the Padre
in the enormous sunset.

A death chant blew
through us like a black knife,
and we could not answer
the echoing well, the abandoned

stones and charred vigas. We couldn't
stake our lives there, to grind our days
in a bowl of red clay,
without water.

Rock dust, grain dust, saw dust, early
    sun licking the mountains
        like a bear's tongue, still
some spike of anger in his shoulder.
        Cant hook, hay hook, meat hook,
          always the whisky-breath
rumour of some border,
    some patch of new ground
        or easy timber.

The ruts go west.
    A raven hauls
        morning's smoky hide
over swamp spruce,
    the radio scratches
        a partly cloudy day.

Never a girl like mom's sweet potatoes.
    So the shy Saskatchewan boy starts rolling
        smokes early, and wanders
from the dugout and bitter fields
    following the greasy harness
        of his dad's last gelding
out of a dead furrow
    and on over the blue summit
        of Alberta
into hemlock darkness, the steep
    green water,
        cedar roots and slough grass
winding west,
    spitting mosquitos and slivers,
        drinking ice melt from a sharp rock
or rye from a cheap label.

He chinks his jack pine shack
    with moss and old underwear
        and traps beaver for tobacco.
The lynx track fills with blood,
    a skinned buck hangs
        from a singletree.

Never spuds creamy like mother's
    or another God-ploughing man
        made of horse bone
to whip him into the stubble.

The last son stays alone
    on the north side of a side creek.
        When the fur drops or runs out
like the best timber he can poach
    he goes downstream
        to tamp railroad ties
or buck loose hay
    to stay thirsty.

Nothing to do but split the ground
    and backbone with an axe—
        cedar into shakes, clay into barley,
spruce into planks, moose into jerky.
    Nothing to do but smack the country
        like a bitch and keep burning
his chest with booze,
    because no sweet potatoes
        can open the fist of his father
now, the dead knuckles against his boy's heart
    numb as a tractor sprocket.

Never a woman
        in all the one-room shacks
                with a tin can stove
some rye and a gallon of jam.
        He drags his boiled coffee and smoke
                and tells me about the boy
who ran away—
        so short of breath now,
                coughing and filing to stubs
the teeth of a rusty crosscut
        that he can make cry
                like wind through a prairie woodshed
or the Cree woman in Winnipeg.
        Tales of threshing gangs, Percherons and steam,
                frozen blankets and his mother
in tears, the homestead furrows
        of snow and grief.

My friend knows things I want
        to know, or almost want to,
                so I keep listening,
wanting to find the hurt kid inside
        this man leaning in thick sleeves
                jammed at the elbows
trying to grind his loneliness
        into chaff and sawdust, stiff hides
                and a pot-metal ashtray.

What keeps any man
        living in a single room?
                Who am I for him? The coffee
is acid, and the old pot warps
        reflections on the table.

I guess he knows I'm thirsty for more
        of the rust and thistles that hammer
                a gyppo down to his last drink.
He knows I came to stay a while.

But if I know the taste
        and odour of this place
                he's burned himself out in,
if I've pressed good steel to the wild
        body I milk and follow
                to a numb pool
I never knew
        the way he came,
                that prairie blurring
as he tells it, blurring out
        ahead of the walking plough
                and the big horse's cracked feet.
I never knew the hands
        of his father, the empty dugout,
                the bugs banging empty days
and nights. I never knew
        the boy I try to find now
                who stumbled west
with a pain he can't wash down.

So I keep listening. How, if he wasn't
        stooking grain, mom had him
                packing turnips and cabbage
to the cellar, or cranking the separator.
        Finally a blizzard came
                that blew him off to war.

Father's horses got sent off
        to the piss barns, or shipped for fox meat,
            the tractor died
against a cottonwood stump,
        the hay turned black
            in the windrow.

Now the rings in every cylinder
        have seized, and nothing
            will fire around here anymore.
It used to be, hell
        if you had a little spark
            and compression
you were away...

Some crossbred steers
        lick the burnt roots
            around his cabin
The shake mill rots
        behind a blown-out Ford
            and a heap of bottles.
The last one cut his throat,
        and he came home with a battery gizmo
            he holds beneath his chin
to make a voice. The saw won't play
        anymore. The coffee and cobwebs aren't the same.
            So what is there to say
now, when I go there
        for the watery-eyed stories
            I could count on?

The wood stove turns cold, and the radio
    scratches a partly cloudy day.
        A few birch leaves
fall on the tilting porch
    where his thin body leans, and his eyes
        have sunk back
to some storm or furrow
    in Saskatchewan.

Sometimes it is harder
    to reach for another man's hand
        than to bleed an animal.

FALL SONG

The ripening grain field swells
    out of aspen shadow
        across the river

another river
    sucking silt
        into its wings

calling geese down
    as all rivers call us
        down from our roads

THE SWEATER

You knitted me this
from the mad curls
of our old ram
I can smell your strong hands
in its darkness
moving deeper
inside this wool
over roots and creek stones
on this mountain
no one ever named it
in the wool's darkness
I still hear you
whisper and try
to tell me where
to find good berries
your soft voice
still wet on the stones
wanting to say
be warm

FOAM

The old logs of the barn
give off a certain odour
of satisfaction, smoke
of musk and mildew.

I have begun to understand
the deep straw, steaming
furrows of daybreak, and my lungs
want the sweetness of jack pine

and manure. My head sweats
against the enormous
flank of the cow we call
Chuckles, as I listen
to the third stomach

rumbling. I feel an ancient stanza
throbbing through the milk vein
as I watch a strange fist flexing,
the same cracked knuckles
fingers and forearm

that lead me up rivers
and into them, that pull me
to gentle bodies, and deeper
into blue clay and moss shadow,

into the delicate windings of blood
and resin. Hand moving ahead of me
with strange dedications, almost out
of reach, contracting like some crude

gland of another body.
Milking.

MAKING WOOD

Wet morning. The fall
mountains have all bled
into the skin of the birch
I'm splitting. The wood
is honey coloured and heavy.

My eyes water in the cold,
so much keeps falling
toward me. The barn
and root cellar are piled full
of all we could pull from the land.

The walls are chinked. Geese calls
bless the river
and the fields,
our shortening days
still high on the banks.

I am ready for winter,
even death,
today.

A shaggy spruce blows its dark
blue wing over a barley field.
The mountain blooms like a purple thistle
behind the farmer wearing a black hat
who grinds and bleaches the day
down to lime and German sausage.

A bear falls out of a cottonwood
and staggers behind the granary,
shot through the ribs.

No stumps anymore. A hog is chewing
the log trapper's shack that is sinking
back to clay, a new barn is crowding the sky.
Boots covered with rooster blood.

My good neighbour drove his family
into the bottomland
with an axe and a Bible.
When the last cedar ashes
were harrowed into stubble
he turned his gelding loose in a slough
and left the salty harness for a porcupine.

My devout neighbour keeps his wife
like a sow. She has given him a beautiful
litter of nine. Daughters bend
down long rows of the garden,
dragging dark clouds. Boys with slim arms
pull a last crop off the field
and shovel steer guts into the manure pile,
snickering at the Lord's work, and at this stranger
come to buy a heifer or green feed from their dad.

Winter, a purple sea piles against the barn,
ammonia steam stains the cold morning.
Inside, the cows stand chained in their heat,
swallowing silage, groaning with tons of harvest
bulging the milk vein, filling the gutter.
Calves bawl and stumble in the dark,
the big stainless tank shines like a coffin.

My neighbour has taught me
when to cut grain and rip
open the earth in fall,
how to look at a Holstein's ass.
He doesn't laugh or remember my name,
the bone is thick around his eyes.
He chops at the steep shadows, at the throat
of wolves, and dumps his garbage in the river.
He can smell boards in a tree
like the fat in a goose.

My stomach is full of barbwire
and bear stew, my butcher's tongue
burns like turpentine.
The farmhouse is full of flies,
and I who tuned my fence to the beaver's tooth
am wading downstream with a snag.

When I turn the hell around
my neighbour croaks with a raven's grin,
Don't ya wanna stay here
and fight the elements…?

There's no shake and goodbye.
Something has thickened his knuckles
so his hand will not open.
He is unloading the silo,
staring at the dull light
off pitchfork tines, a numbness
climbing hardwood grain to his shoulders
where the fear of God throbs like a tractor.

1.

We went out to hack open the day like a fat calf or a tree
We went out to rake the earth of mice and low-nesting birds
We went out to dig the veins of the black bear
We went out to the meadows that floated like women or low clouds
We startled geese on the sandbars
We went out rolling huge rubber tires, carrying wrenches forged
       from rusted flutes and moose ribs
We went out into the wet arms of dawn while coyotes still called
       over the river
The air was tart as crab apple and cool and the fields rolled
       in their mist, luminous as salmon
       in the first pools of light
We went out while our kids were whispering in their sleep
       like willows above a creek
We went out to taste berries against the barbwire
We went out to make hay
We went out with Jersey cream on our lips, jerky in our pockets
       and bear fat on our boots
Out through the gate as the shores of darkness were sinking
Damp smoke rippled toward us from deer and our cattle
We went out to rub the resins of pine and incense of red cedar
       on our bodies and drink
       the heavy brandy of stumps
We went out to swath and bale the first flesh of daylight
       pushing our shoulders in circles
       while an eagle scissored the sky
       her flight always changing the borders
       we imagined
We went out with booms and spindles, harrows and seed drills
       choppers and high carbon teeth
       out with hammers and rivets
       and cold meat sandwiches

We went out to cut the long hair of Smohalla's woman where only
    a few wet braids of Shuswap fishermen had been
    camped beside the rack of drying salmon
We listened on the riverbank by a leaning spruce where Yellowhead
    had watched the slapping beavers
We blew the match a drunk brakeman dropped into the duff
    so the railroad could come through
    and we watched the animals run up side creeks
    with their fur on fire
We went out with marten traps, pitchforks and rum
We rode up Goat River, Castle Creek, The Beaver, Swift Current,
    Horse Creek, Tenmile, Ptarmigan, Buck Creek,
    Slim Creek, the Big and Little Shuswap,
    snapping alders, mud oozing to the girth
    chasing a moose with twin calves
    across the river into black spruce
We went out to skin the lynx and toss barley at the moon
We were thirsty for the liquor of clay and silt, juice of timothy
    brome grass and clover that swelled
    round our tractor wheels
We drove our horses our tractors our families in circles
    at the foot of Yuh-hai-has-kun
    Mountain of the Spiral Road
We went out to set chokers around the great spruce
    while red squirrels yelled down
    through the hail of cones
We went out to bulldoze the yellow fog between cottonwood
    trunks, and then we hacked up the trunks
    and burned them with diesel and truck tires
When the smoke cleared and the last charred bone was tilled
    under, we admired the harrowed field
    that glistened in the purple silence
    like a great pelt

We cursed and twisted the last roots of bottomland
      into wire rope, worm gears and pork chops
      until the sun was hung like a new carcass
      in a cedar snag
We went out in baseball caps and rubber boots
      and our watches wound tight until they froze
      and fell from our wrists
We went out full of coffee, with latigo leather cinched around
      our stomachs, our hearts full of bacon
      our knuckles like dog teeth
We went out while the smoke from our cabins rose
      straight as a spike
      between the mountains
We went out while the women refilled kettles
      and stirred the coals
      out while they washed Mason jars
      and hung cabbages and cheeses in the cellar
      out while they gathered
      herbs and plucked the chickens
When will you come back, they asked, *when do you think*
      you might come back
      the women wondered
We went out to buckle heavy harness on the mountains
      that smelled sweet as lemon
      our lungs big as silos
      our faces red as beef
We went out to find more earth we could drain
      slough we could graze or plough open
We went out to spit blueberry juice at the storm of mosquitos
Sometimes the ripe windrows unwound like lovers
      sometimes like entrails
We went out to the ruts and the breakdowns
      and the coughing animals

We went out for the distance, to look back
        at the peeled logs we had chinked with violence
        the walls we had hewn to keep us
        away from the women
We went out to pump grease into sprockets
        and kingpin bushings
We went out because it was out and it was endless
        the green day was endless
While salmon crowded to the mouths of clear rivers
        we went out
        we went up the rivers we had named
        and hung them with steel and timber trusses
We put the virgin clay in barges, the new crop in wagons
        the milk of Han Shan's cold mountain
        in stainless tanks
We went out to make hay
We went out without forgiveness
We went out before the raven climbed into his ragged pulpit
        out before the owl digested her weasel
We went out to make wood, to split open birch and red cedar
        we went out for the taste of heartwood
When are you coming back, the women whispered, *maybe you*
        could guess

2.
We went out to yank the breaking plough down
        through the slough, rolling
        up peat like dark liver
        from under the deep grass
We went out with good steel on our tongues
We went out with barrels of diesel and hydraulic oil
        out with dried fruit and bullets in our trousers

We kept a jug of spring water tied near the drawbar
        a jug of rum or dandelion wine
        stashed in the granary
We went out when the milk was sweet, to crush the green light
        in our fists and mouths
We went out to plough the land we loved in its wildest hours
        as we would have loved our women
We went out to hurt
We went out to cobble and tighten a row of contraptions
        as the glacier began blowing sails into the sun
We went out on the path of Calvin
        and all the storybooks after Cooper
We went out through wild roses and fireweed
        without reading Wang or Walt Whitman
We went out among the nostrils of blue horses
The fields rippled naked and gentle, and we went to them
        as we would have gone to our women
We churned ruts to the river, riprapped the banks
        and kept circling the land
        we were burning, stretching
        galvanized wire, driving staples
        even when there was nothing
        to hold
We flushed grouse and rabbits from saskatoon bushes, bearberry
        and dogwood, slashed and filled gullies
        until they were level enough
        for the mower
We tumbled stumps across the valley
        until no cover was left, no draws
        full of quivering shadow for animals
        to find the river

Before we ran out of ground, before we came to shallow
    water widening in fir darkness
    we opened the throttle
    to hear the last trunks snap like kindling
    under the blade and grousers
When we lit the piles of forest they hissed
    and cracked, the flames rose
    up the valley, and our smoke
    blew off between the wind-chiseled blue peaks
We went out to heap burnt roots, boulders and scrap iron
    into anonymous caves and solitudes
We went to stay out
We tuned our barbwire fences like banjoes
    or sometimes like cellos
    beneath the aspens
We went out to wring the rooster into a dark furrow
We went out to make hay
We went out to shovel potatoes soaked with hog's blood
    out to the sheds where no language is possible
We went out because our male hands trembled when they met
We went out to break our bodies
    while the tractor belched clods
    of diesel smoke into the clear morning
We hauled and hauled on the fields, drunk on alfalfa
    green chop, barley and clover blossom, cries
    of geese and ospreys, sun dogs
    and the altitude
We packed and tarped the bunker
    and gloated over the great fermentation
    while a mountain of shit smoked
    beside the milking parlour

Our faces burned raw in the buckshot wind of chaff and straw,
        sawdust, sand and grasshoppers
There was always more land coming toward us
            forest and willow bog, breaking like green surf
            in the chaotic sun
            always stones floating up with weeds
            to the surface
We cranked the ropes of the sun around a stump
            and swallowed the river clay
We drove a heavy pipe into the moss of Native dead
            and snickered as it poured
            wheat into the boxcars
We pulled manure wagons into the heat to dump slurry
            on daisies and wild strawberries
We pulled the life up out of the swamps, heavy
            green bladders full of sap and turpentine
            and we punctured them to make hay
Our silage smouldered like sauerkraut, and the cows' udders
            bulged in our hands like bread dough
We baled the sweetness of the deepest land, heaving summer
            upon summer into rotting feed bunks
While the porcupine dozed in a lodgepole
            and the hawk climbed a thermal screw
            we watched our crankcase ink spread
            over the open ground
When the dust of the harvest rose, we watched
            our loaded barns and silos leaning
            into the blurry horizon
We heard the axle snap between our shoulders
            as storm gathered in the limbs of afternoon

3.

We went out, as the saying goes,
        with our hearts in our hands
What else can a man do, but go out with whatever he is
            feeling in his hands
            and work it out
Out to sweat against the tug of high water
            the dark unbroken land
            a little fire in our shoulders
Out, as the Jesus-jumping neighbour says, *to fight the elements*
Red slivers, char and mica, mud and intestines
            the dark sod sliced to ribbons
            the rusty pickup full of barley
            the knuckles numb as roller bearings
Out to the paddock full of steers, the broken
            iron scattered and sinking
            at the borders, the wet
            land drained of ducks and seeded
            down to grass, the coyote hung stiff
            on a fence post
Better to stop doubt at the wrists, keep the unspeakable
            blue stones from climbing up
            the arm veins
Better to stop the hunger at our wrists, keep some desires
            in the fist
Dig to the headwater roots at the face
            of a mountain, under the sledgehammer sun
            twist the rainbow light
            down into a stump
            like a rooster's neck

Go out to the meadows that float like women
        or low clouds, groggy
        with the exhaust of machinery
        out to the breakdowns
        and coughing animals
Out to the sheds
        where no language
        is possible

4.
We fought muskeg and gophers, shear pins, pulleys and carburetors
        while a raven was swinging in our shadow
        splitting the air with its sarcastic laugh
        mocking the fever of our need
We went out to squeeze vinegar from devil's club and thistle
        and we loved the acid on our tongues
We went out to drag the fleece from our ewes and cut
        the balls and horns off our cattle
We went out to make meat
We went out to bleed the animals we milked and loved
        we called them by name
        and threw their hides over the jack pine corral
The air was heavy with pollen and a few slow clouds
        and we went out to taste berries
        against the barbwire
We went out to make hay
While the river was swelling to the mudsills
        our fence rails were already collapsing
        the new borders burning and floating
        away from us
We went out and could not turn back
        until the haymow glowed like honeycomb
        and fire smouldered in the fallow wakes of dusk

We would not turn until the ridges of dust purpled and froze
        against our shoulders, and we remembered
        the laughter of our kids
Not until the tractor sank in the field
        and darkness rippled behind a beaver
        could we remember where the day began
        or think of turning around
The backwater was filling with shadow, and a blue heron
        pulled the barn full of swallows
        downriver toward night
We worked with our backs to the mountains
        waiting for the limestone cliff to crack
        like a wolf's jaw
        the lunar fuse and auroras
        to arc and vibrate subarctic night
Our eyes burned like gasoline to see fall coming
        to watch the alpine whiten
        and push the moose with frost in his antlers
        down the mountain
When we could no longer see the flash of the sickle
        or the wake of new hay behind us
When we could just smell only smell what we'd made
        and taste the cool dusk falling
        on our forearms
We shut off the tractor
        and the river began
        rising toward us

5.
Smell the last honey of cottonwoods
Smell the whole day like steam from a well
        or a fresh stump inside us

Pitch and blood, bodies stained with clay and pulp juice
    of the day shot through our knuckles
If we wanted something more, it was too dark now
        to tear it out of the ground
When we stopped burning shafts and ball bearings, pounding
        brass and cast iron, stopped tightening belts
        and roller chains, feeding bales to the mow
        and grain to the hopper
When we stopped making ruts in the earth to make hay
        and there was no more sheet metal to tear
        no more rope or rubber or nerve to fray
We could begin to smell what we made of ourselves
        the heat and mineral of clay
        seed and straw smouldering like a fist in our lungs
        the odour of cattle in our shirts
        the grease and pollen on our hands
We spit into a dead furrow and turned, we watched darkness
        walking up the rifle barrel
We could taste the river on our lips
        and we were thirsty for something
        we could not reach
        or name
We couldn't bang any more out of the ground
        or split open another tree
        it was too late
        to make anything
The river was drinking our land
        drinking the borders we imagined
If we wanted something else, maybe
        we were too tired to know
        or too groggy to ask

Whatever we thought was ours after all—
        old-growth logs ripped open,
        green bales crammed to the rafters,
        hams hanging in the smokehouse—
        may not have been all
        we wanted
It was late now, a few geese circled the still flood water
        and sunken fields, the heavy basalt wings of mountains
        were folding under the widening night
We turned around, following a tractor rut
        and sagging barbwire to the house
How hungry are you
        we could hear them asking.

HAYFIELD

The grass is so deep still,
moving under the wind
like the big mare
we could not ride.

Neither she nor this wild meadow
will come to us again.
They find each other
now, as we had wanted

and together become a wave
at dusk, washing away
from our sheds
and our sorrow

and the wagon tracks
like two warped bones
still sinking
in the sea we chopped open.

OVERSLEEPING

Riffles on the eddy
    aspen limbs breathing
        so early on the wall

look into this
    shaky mirror
        full of knots

get up
    and wash in the river
        old boy

from

Iron Fever

Stylish and gourmet, impetuous to cook and serve the raw
while foreclosing and parceling the last park-pruned wild,
we notch and mortise the coast into a sequence
of rapturous views. So here again, another headland
is mortgaged by the broker of caviar vacations,
old ranch land lavishly groomed and oiled
for mimosa mornings.

A wine cork's toss
from miles of tinted plate glass walls
and exotic joinery, beside the blooming
jogger's path, at the edge of a foam-battered promise
of paradise, where homestead barn planks and pickets
rot in wild iris, a sign reads AREA UNDER
RESTORATION.

Which is to say, here is where bankers
and corporate gunmen stroll in romance, the over-privileged
in rubber suits bob and paddle through glossy kelp, snorkel
for the last abalone, frolic in dream coast "dog holes"
where drunk schooner skippers once heaved in
against smoking rocks and took the virgin
liver-dark lumber away in the fog.

GALLERY OPENING
(after García Márquez)

What am I doing here again
among the Italian leather
loafers, handmade gold
jewelry, conceptual
art and facelifts?

Through the tall plate glass
California hills cook brown
and wrinkle like mummies
or an old mestizo face
in the realtor's vineyard.

Perhaps like you I came to sneak
a little taste of sushi
and the realtor's grapes,
see if I could swim
among the waxed lips

of virtual imagination.
But I keep hearing Balthazar
moan in the mud and dog shit
outside a smoky pool hall
in Mexico, T-shirt soaked

with cerveza, his parrot cage
long since smuggled north and lost,
the drunk dawn scratching
pig blood above tin roofs,
a scraggly rooster and a nun

bending over him, mumbling
some religious bribe
into his ribs, before he wakens
from a nightmare
of fatuous decoration.

How many would memorize some Yeats just
to get laid? And how would you have guessed
a rented plastic canoe would put your Alaskan sea skills
to the test? When you finally pushed off
from the flimsy dock, a little end-rhyme heat on, the paddle
looking clumsy enough for her to ask, *Can you
paddle?*, like a poet you stuttered back
to calm her, "I've been on the water
all my life."

Still close to shore, *Innisfree* began to go blank
in your forked-horn head. Maybe just
for the sake of poetics, you managed
to grab some blackberries off the prickly bank
with only a wobble. But when she lifted her jersey
and rubbed blackberry juice on her nipples
your seamanship was on the line, suddenly
a little too high above the waterline.

It was a flat-bottom canoe,
but her boobs
and the dark juice
rocked everything.
You lunged for a weeping
willow as the craft flipped.
And saved yourselves
for poetry.

DOC SAYS

If you live between windy cow towns
where the grub is greasy, and the sidewinding waitress
with a rodeo buckle under her winking navel
complains to a big hat hay hauler at the counter
she hasn't been fishing for two damned weeks—

that's probably why you moved here,
not for the prime rib and range wars,
or even Barb in her tight Wranglers,
but because you know how good the country is
by how greasy the food is.

Sitting high getting high in the yellow
cab wiggling five to fifty tons of turbo-
charged iron with your magic black
fingers one hand fiddling
your balls one greasy hand tickling
the valve sticks deaf drunk on diesel
sweet hiss and moan of hydraulics
ripping open the earth with a hard-
face bucket rock teeth hard-on Caterpillar bull
dozer blade screeching sprockets chrome boom
rams shining in the roaring sun five
fingers man on the cock knob levers
high pressure hot oil lines jumping
jesus this is some kind of *mutha*
fucking fun

A few miles inland from the salt boiling
headland dog holes and purple rock spines
where schooners heaved in for the last
load of virgin first growth, saws revving
in sword fern creek beds, Pomo house pits
full of duff, acorn mush gone black
as newts and gear grease, over a hundred years
of misery whips and big cables, old-growth stumps
too big for the old boys to burn through
second growth suckers circle the ghosts
winch around 'em, get what you can

Air sticky sweet with fir sap, throat stings
with tree acid, chopper's blood half stump molasses
half turpentine liquor, hot afternoon skidding trees
through deep clay powder, gotta be some dope
in this red dust, turkey vultures eating skunk meat
way down at the farmhouse switchback, gotta be
some forgiveness, guys trying to make a buck
in the woods, anyway where in hell
did your gingerbread come from, chrome
thermos cup on a new stump, shirt soaked
with diesel, big T-bone grin

Loader grapple shines, saw logs decked high
pushing six loads a day, damn good ground now
good wood, but hey guys
a few termites flying around, pretty soon clouds
crawling down from Alaska, red mud
plugging the undercarriage, sprockets buried
gyppo can't get it into high gear
soon enough.

Drain oil drips down like sweet molasses
into his mustache, into his eye; trickles
down his throat for a lifetime. Tarot faces
in the drain pan, I-Ching in the lug nuts rolled out
in black gravel on a roadside.

Digging bearing grease out of the wheel hub
like blueberry jam, pig shit, or salsa—the bones
and veins of a man that hungry, that given
to the jacked up broken beast, his mind and his wrenches
moving in circles, heart licking carbon
cocktails from his knuckles, that hungry
for the rig to run right, that turned on
as we say, by the sweet click of a ratchet
as the world is torqued and tuned
to some manageable shudder
and vibration, the *sonabitch*
ready to rip loose some last good
hunk of big sky real estate, fueled up
and greased for "harvesting."

Come winter, a few kicks and a little blast of ether
will get the frozen iron to shake and belch—*for cris'sake*
and get rolling out into the cloudless
pink daybreak, all the nameless acres
of a man's dream cut wide open now
and hung with steel, slough meadow and clearcut
stretched and nailed down like a salted hide.

Gotta be some dope cookin
in that crankcase, pal.

The raptor's predatory glide and swoop is surely etched
into the bone and jelly of a man's skull, the infinite
choreography of plunge and pirouette charged into nerve
cells and filaments of hunter, artist, athlete, dancer and physician.

The master's oily brush stroking light and skin blush into blank
canvas, a neurologist's stainless blade and needle beneath
the scalp, the twisting airborne lay-up or leaping end-zone catch,
Romero's electric fingers on the flamenco strings and frets;

nothing less than Leonardo's hands, the Inuit's ulu slicing
open a seal on sea ice, or a slick dealer's slippery shuffle
of the deck. What travels through the fishline miracles
of nerves from pupil to muscle and tendon

to articulate action into flesh or vibrating air, Italian marble
or virgin earth, the brain's animal grace and motive burns
like a liquid fuse into human hands, hands that chisel
contrapposto into a pietà, or polish the limestone balls

of some Greek god. Like the falcon's talons, hands devoted
to good work execute the artful. No less swift and elegant
than surgeon or sculptor is the man fondling hydraulic valves,
moving earth, digging holes and trenches with such economy,

precision and grace, you would send him to Rome
or Florence with canonical privilege and appointments
to excavate new foundations and sewers for the classical
temples, turrets and arenas, send him also with master blueprints

to smouldering Amazonia, or rush him to Mars, let the galactic
digging begin. The surest reading of geologic volumes
and tensions flickers in his eye. Like harpsichord keys
the tractor levers twitch and move, the ground opens

to a precise partita he composes new each time, virtuoso
hands so delicately guiding tons of heavy metal, the earth
so perfectly cut open, we marvel and know in our groins
god loves a blue-eyed man who digs a beautiful hole.

You were curling up against the firewall
hours past bedtime with a ratchet inhaling high lead
liquor and carbon of the flathead fondling pistons
rods and guides in love with the perfect closures of rings
and valves the taste of oil getting sweeter
than grandma's fruit pies the cold engine swallowing
every mystery outside a boy's body outside
the garage the stucco neighbourhood outside
the night so damned quiet you would drink anything
suck gas from a siphon hose badass burn
of ethyl or cheap whisky in your throat
love that sting drink anything
to hot rod shudder the world hot shit
scare a dumb town crazy with the lope
of your radical cam the rap of those glasspacks
and burning rubber down main street past midnight
where in hell is anything
shaking.

Warm plum of the stick shift knob
in your sweaty palm the hiss and suck
of carbs guzzling hell out of Friday night
no hood on your coup those shiny dual
or triple gas pots chrome headers peacock blue
lacquered fenders frenched headlights
ploughing back the store fronts.

*

The first touch of the flathead V-8 cylinder wall
was slippery as a girl's tongue the first one you felt
safe enough to get it on with going down
sweaty between moon hubcaps
beneath the big fuzzy dice

Fingers in the distributor or twisting the jet screw whatever
secrets you were feeling for trying to get it
timed right and idling whatever Tabasco taste
of booze or gasoline bit the base of your skull

like a rattler fang whatever fear would do
would drink you were resolving spirit
and matter at intersections in the lurch
and squeal of second-gear rubber or beneath
the hood on the intake manifold
or under the wishbone with a wrench

Before you could claim your own
boy body fruit fuzz banana smell boy muscles
or hear your own name spoken out
in a big room before a pimple
or whisker any proof any handle
on anything you crawled in with hoses
pistons shafts and head bolts torque-

wrenching your first solitudes
crawled up and down the dark chassis
greasing the nipples loving the snap
and ooze of grease popping out seals
and loose bushings.

Hair greased trousers creased hardtop waxed
like a dark mirror you drank whatever
you had to get into her blouse get parked get hot
get down in the tuck-and-roll on that static tune
behind the dashboard of your lacquered Merc
enough of anything to put a quick fuse
into your spine a quick flame
to fear and confusion keep your drop axle candy apple
coup loud and low nothing but blacktop moving
underneath nothing but motion
the volume cranked to no pain cruising
in your Naugahyde bucket R & B vibrating
the night ripping the headliner
everything out over the hood shaking
loose.

Our towers of gears and hydraulics, chain sprockets,
buckets, booms and levers—the endless excavation,
drilling and pumping, the craters, clearcuts, open pits,
dams and slag heaps—has all this phallic irreverence
and fever been a predestined affliction—all these
fabulous contraptions the mad extensions
of our opposable thumb, the spear arm flexing
for a hundred thousand years, taut with some
impossible hunger, the carved tusk and obsidian driven
deeper under fallen moons, a man's empty fist raging
against coiled vines and jaguar claws of night
beyond the flickering shadow wall?
Are the shining shafts and cables a man's tendons
stretched to their inevitable labours after fire
and copulation and the mammoth
bones sucked empty?

Hot liquor of diesel and throb of pistons, sweet steel
machine, meadow and rock mountain cut open
for the deep vibration and taste of dominance, hammered
kidneys and spine, the man with swollen hands going deaf
in a yellow cab—could one have read it
in the etched vault of stone, a desire invisible
in smoky petroglyphs and calcium fragments,
in a broken skull's wormed calligraphy, or the little pile
of obsidian flakes among burnt stones?

Could one have imagined Europe's forests gutted, the stench
and smoke of wild carcasses blackening heavens
of one hemisphere, then another, the low lands
and prairies ripped open like sheep, the steaming coasts
sloshing red with sawdust and whale blood,
mountains flushed with monitor nozzles,
buffalo tongues and black liver of river valleys
buried under the rubble of cities, a white man's jaw full
of gold teeth, biting a dark nipple—could anyone
have seen the first whittled bone
and black stone blade in a man's nervous hand
doing *this*?

SONG COMES

[when] we who are small
will feel even smaller...
—Orpingalik, Inuit shaman

Sky tumbled with rim-rock scree, lichen-brushed
fault scarp rising from mirrors of water birds
into cougar skin bunchgrass mesa, lava nippled,
juniper stubbled, badger clawed. Winding butte,

slumped caldera, burning plateau—with a hawk's or raven's taste
for the planet's igneous undulations, steep terrors, and vast
fragrance, you ride into great cloud-hammered convergences
with the fragile nerves of a digger squirrel and the gratitude

rush of the red-tail that just swallowed you. Not quite
a raptor's thermal *contrapposto*, but the horizontal
torque of your curious Cro-Magnon meandering
through basin and range on rubbery lugs, in a mirage

of antelope, a wash of silver sage, your proprietary delusions
and sufferings sucked from your song socket, charred
clean and anonymous once again—as if a fist of obsidian
ripped into your belly and lungs, and flung you again

with your hunger for emptiness even farther
into Miocene distances, alkali blown, pocked and sharp-antlered,
swallow-kissed, rattler-drilled.

A linguist calls it the Axis
of Substitution, this
affliction you're following

as my head goes bobbing
through greasewood and gnarled
rock of desert stream beds,

reaching for an obsidian flake,
coyote bone, or juniper root
to whittle into a new analogy.

CORE TESTING

If suffering puts root hairs
into a hardening mesh of nerves

that swells into an invisible
weight hanging on the torso

the way burl or conk bulges on a tree
trunk—some milky dream fluid gone wild

bird's-eye or grey and rubbery, pulling the body
slightly off to one side … If the heart had rings

and you could stare into the stump
before falling, maybe you could tell

from its simple labour, when craving
kinks veins and ganglia into blind

pockets, maybe you could reach in, hear
the hours pumping, pinch the soft amber

marbles of blood, and taste
the citrus of nothingness.

Sometimes you are given mountains
as a boy, sapwood to breathe, dark
stones with a thousand faces

and spring water to follow.
Sometimes you are given a boat,
a green morning made of shadows

and no one beside you
for days, or years. I'm not sure
Love what you have to do

with all this. I was given
a wild place to be. Sometimes
it hurt to move out there

as evening rippled, and no voice
came back from the animals.
Sometimes now

when you travel alone or beside me
your silence frightens me
on the naked water.

I put my knife in a tree
as a boy, began carving a good story
to winter in. I can go back

and back there, wait for the osprey's cry,
let sunlight open and close my hands,
and risk nothing with you.

Or stay here without knowing
if I'm somewhere upstream, or climbing
through leaves without a name,

this wild touch of yours—
I'm tasting mountains
for the first time.

WINDSHAKE

Look into a stump
or sunrise

rings leaking syrup
or cloudy rum

lips wet with resins
clock with no hours

look in the mouth
of laughter

face without numbers
under the eyelids

some lives will not root
in geometry

or hold anything
but the coastal

edges
of rivers and tides

after you count the rings
and sap clots

look for the hairline
split in the heart

the crack
wind opens

in the dark
center.

LOVER

Without syntax or hyperbole,
gently reaching, you have come closest
to the source of my hands, and lingered

sometimes in devotion, as a rivulet
has known the stones and alder roots
in its falling.

Crowberries: New Poems

I

I followed your ruts
through sand and mud, ground them
deeper, while sundogs and raptors
drifted over wild rye and greasewood,
playas and fault scarps.

Schist and obsidian sparkled
where a rattler crossed my track.
It took so little
to keep my throat from burning.
Antelope left a mirage of willow

and cottonwood honey floated up
out of creek bottoms, soft breeze
like a woman's breath. Who could remember
the day or crumpled map at the bottom
of one's panniers?

Camped under wind-carved rim rock
or blue juniper, sometimes a rivulet's
liquor and music, so much wild
meat and coyotes always
following my fires.

Nearing the Cascades or Sierras, sawtooth
horizons purpled and rippled with a promise
I was afraid to sing of. Lurching
through volcanic jaws and deadfall
into dark hemlock and cedar

under curtains of mist, horsetails and skunk
cabbage grabbed my belly, almost
swallowed everything. Still I followed your ruts
through peat and clay, silt and gravel,
churned them deeper.

The packrat has stashed   peach pits shriveled apples
horse turds and mushrooms   on the manifold of my pickup
where he must be thinking   winter will blow under
my axles with no hassle   no cold cranking
or frivolous runs   to the village.

Though we hardly speak   a quiet and sarcastic collaboration
grows between us   some crudely digested
haiku and pithy complaints   long before solstice
grips the old fruit trees   and buries my truck hubs
dark pellets of poetry   cover the carburetor.

Affliction

Deep purple curtains
drag the playa over miles
of sage and greasewood.
Men drill their hope and hunger
down dry wells and rattler holes.

*

What Would the Roshi Say?

Thistles and rusting
tractor prop the sagging barn,
sunrise rippling orange.
Crane cries fill the Void.
You can drop your hammer now.

*

Above the Cabin

Another season
rusts and warps against the bone
that carves my song lines.
Turning in aquamarine light
a necklace of water birds.

*

October First

Chill enough to start
a fire and turn the page
for another month,
shuffle leaves and old song lines,
watch the veins rise on my hand.

*

Religious Ends

The barns keep falling
into rust heaps and thistle.
Old cowboys spit blood.
The ranch orchard still smoulders
while they widen the highway.

*

Hang On

Wind turning bitter.
How many old truck tires will it take
to hold your tin roof down?

*

Frost and Lung Smoke

The hard land sparkles.
Five does are watching two bucks
cracking horns in a stubble field
beside the dry stream bed where I
pause my jogging. The does appear
casually amused.

*

New Year's Morning

Broken squirrel teeth click
under fresh snow, wild tracks
criss-crossing my empty mind.
Blue drift buries my song breath.
Old packrat stole my truck keys.

Pale rose, apple blush faded, old tractor
roughly my age, still running smooth, no blue
smoke, and surely it will outlive me; maybe my children

also. It's about low RPM's, heavy castings
and simplicity. One of the last ones. Iron poured out
with an obsolete notion of longevity

and bottomland's redemption, belief that God's smouldering
furrows promised righteous pain and divinity
in the grain field and the foundry.

Iron poured out with rough knuckles
and somnolent delusion, red glow gone but sure
to outlast my solitary dream of harvests, sure to plough

under new dream revisions—the last ones with old songs
still cracking in my hands. So I mutter
to my trusted cold contraption that mocks

with the smoothest idle my stuttering breath
and ligaments, this integrity of heavy iron
that survives fruit and fermentations will go on

ripping hard ground under windfall shadow, turning
plum pits, duff and deadwood into fruit blush, as now,
pausing to reach up from the tractor seat, I pull down

the last red ones through a purpling afternoon,
as sandhill cranes crank the heavens, and the cold
tractor idles like a ghost beneath me.

Grief is a badger. His hole
is clawed between sharp rocks, miles out
in igneous country under twisted juniper
and burning greasewood. Hardly ever
found in the shade of apple or willow roots.

Born the size of a shrew or baby's fist
in the spiny dark of some storm night
in high desert silt or scree, when the fiery
first milk of early spring sky is suddenly
shattered like obsidian over calderas.

What's it like gripping small bones
and gravel under silver sage
and bunchgrass, sharing the volcanic
dark with rattlers and digger
squirrels, hungry witness to so much
frenetic zigzagging of rabbits
and packrats under the heavy wings
of eagles and migrating cranes?

One's teeth and claws grow sharp
from living in the dark, then gradually
dull from digging in desert gravel
and coyote bones. Grief sweetens solitude
when you understand abandonment,
waken alone among the pulsing
veins of fossil water, licking the sulfurous
heat rising up from fissures of black rock.

Ask while trimming your moustache
or rinsing rat fur from your mouth,
is my badger dreaming or grinding snake meat
in his steamy cradle of stones, is he coming up
to snuffle some joy in the blossoming rabbit brush,
or cramped up again below in bones and burnt muscle
clawing under your heart, too drunk on sour blood
to push the scraps and shards out of his salty doorway?
Will you croon him pity or forgiveness
or lure him up to daylight with fresh roadkill?

Crimson bonbons thrust
up through beaten horse pasture,
sagebrush, clay and stones—

spiked torch gorgeously
hostile, solitary barbed stranger
ignoring the stubborn years

when we hammered hard country
with rusty machines
and bitter coffee.

Obsidian scatter and coyote bones
in the alkali silt under my boots,
raucous old raven leading me back uphill
past the steaming hot spring to empty
eagle nests in chiseled rim rock, and on
into a juniper stubbled caldera.
                              How can I
translate the blunt syllables of this
old priest of emptiness who chops the wind
over miles of playa and dry bunchgrass hummocks,
fallen homestead rails and broken iron, winding
over abandoned ruts and rusty barbwire,
truck ruts I swore I wouldn't leave
but did regardless?

Regardless, I drove deeper, and drove away
antelope and eagles from their spring nesting,
eager to rip up sage and greasewood, hack out a spread
like western books I'd read, hold off the ghost
of a hunter who left his smoke and stories
under the rock ledge beside a shrinking lake bed,
hunter who drug a carcass through wild rye
and rabbit brush a thousand years ago.
Lungs full of larkspur and cottonwood honey,
he may have made his way with a song,
he may have moved in silence, he may have called
the raven down to his fire.

Stubble fields and playa hammered by wind, dry
horizon sliced open by raptor wings, stretched wide
from caldera to rim rock
by antelope hooves and coyotes,

lungs filling again with sage and juniper sap,
alkali dust, wild plum, sweet acid on the slick blue stone
of solitude, sometimes a quick song line
stolen from a magpie, the cracked road
sometimes blurring a little
beyond miles of sagging barbwire.

In the chill turning light, gold rippling
of rabbit brush and cottonwood plumes,
cobalt lake mirror shriveling below
the empty road, road that cuts through fault scarp
and willow slough, salt and sweetgrass, a purple
horizon stretching beyond grief and memory, pulling me
into the last straightaway.

Gold light shattering the last
cottonwoods and willow ravines,
flooding bitterbrush and grasslands, wind ripping
the homestead beneath purple cloud and wakes of fire.
Always enough roadkill for the magpie
and coyote who keeps running beside
my pickup, always another warped barn
collapsing around a curve, and a raven
pounding the emptiness above cracked alkali
playa, greasewood and ghost juniper,
the same raven you can trust to stay
ahead and wake you up at the end of the road.

Above the hot spring where immigrants lost
their horses, where their families scraped hides
and scalded chickens, a rock bluff
the colour of dried blood juts from shale
coyote shit and stud piles. The eagle nests
are empty now, left for the raven
who is somersaulting ahead of me
in a bitter wind.

Umber desert rolls
away, wild grass and greasewood,
sage and playa. The breath of emptiness
abandons the land and its shadows,
abandons lives that scratched and dug here,
souls that kept dreaming
beneath sparkling black holes
until the wind took them.

Great Basin endless and magnificent, clouds
unimaginable. Because you know the winds
so well, my Love, were you beside me, you could tell me
what is brewing in the vault
beyond the volcanic mountains.

II

Old black bears stash meat
in duff to rotten sweeter.
Grandma makes plum jam.
Grandpa peels full moon onion,
bites deeper into poem.

Too much stump syrup
tractor grease grain chaff in head
to write a poem.
Strange wild tracks on the stream bank—
maybe they'll scratch my song lines.

*

No slivers will get you
to move off this old-growth slab
of redwood, dark-oiled
bird's-eye throne, wide enough
for a big ass and notepad.

*

Outhouse door swung wide
lets spring cottonwood perfume
into brain, swelling
river starts sucking my fields
away, riprap won't hold them.

*

Outhouse door swung wide
open, so farmer can gaze
at burnished saw-tooth
mountains. Bee from below stings
end of cock, cold beer can soothes.

What reptile won't leave
its dead skin behind
on a hot stone?

Clinging to old stories
you feel the vellum
grip your throat.

The rattler's eyes
get cloudy as he knows
the past is slipping

down his spine
into silt
and volcanic dust

where we also
twist and leave
our stories.

1.

When you're out there
in frozen woods at night
in heavy boots or snowshoes
and suddenly some sparks fly by
you want to know the source
follow them back
to the fire
burning in a stranger's camp
heartwood flame
without a face.

2.

The jungle hunter
cuts darkness and silence
with a naked blade
comes back to a grass hut
brings a monkey home to eat
makes love in his hammock
living on what we call dark
edges but in the center
of poetry
with no tool or need
to write it down—
when you have to
write it down
the source is drying up.

He kept winding farther into gentle country
beyond the governor's raw ear and his fading harangues,
and his silk bag kept swelling with poems
slapping the donkey's flank, neither the drunk man
nor his burden caused the beast to stumble,
but long before he reached his hut
beyond the noise of men, his stuffed bag of verses
surely split and scattered poetry
with donkey apples among the brilliant colours
of fall.
   And surely as we fill the finely woven
bag of our afflictions while bending to read damp leaves
left by a stubborn old Chinese poet and the intoxicating breath
beneath, we know our hut of solitude is near, we'll trust
that enough has fallen gently through our hands
among the noise of men, and much we've scattered behind
with the ink and bray of our animal joy and loneliness
will compost in a song of leaves, we can trust
this was always the right trail and donkey path
into a silent country.

CROWBERRIES

Wings slicing thick cloud
over the purpling mountain
circle my shadow.

Quick breath stings my lungs.
As the trail steepens, our creek camp
blurs into smoke far below.

Thankful the body's ropes
refuse to fray, my heart's thirst
finds the tiniest fruit among stones.

III

HOME

There were no Jeep tracks
to the stones we first drank from,
no scrap iron rusting.

Four grizzlies greeted us
in green slough meadow
by a sinking trapper's shack.

We all rolled in the deep grass ·
and said goodbye, before we knew
we had come too late.

So soon across the river
a big diesel growling, trees snapping,
ravens twisting. The dark wild

we brought our babies to
so quickly piled and smoking.
The years we've wept.

Your clear breath keeps turning
each page on this dark flight
above the coldest rivers, keeps holding
the hours that remain on a journey
through black wind we share with migrants
in the moon before morning.

with her brush, the artist
touches one part of her life
with another.
—from *Braided Creek*, Kooser & Harrison

Or swirls them into one
life, single unbroken journey
into a wild confluence of rivers and clouds,
boulders, bones and glaciated earth,
steady brush in her hand
filling the most urgent solitude,

tracking dreams of bears, and ghosts
of caribou through jagged firmaments, smoke
and tundra, rivers of stone, ridge after glacial
flow and valley, climbing with no one
beside her, no one to pause or break
her course or hush the wind beneath her.

*

Over muskeg, ice fields and migrations
her Super Cub floating subarctic air,
curling thin cloud and climbing, no one
near, nothing to turn her south
or slow her solo flight
through darkening winds and smoky skies.

Country no one owns, no one holds, she knows
and gathers in her blood until it burns from her hands
with lyric and dirge, shadows of a thousand flights
through ice winds of wolf and raven, rainbow light
of glaciers, fires and auroras, echo of boulders
and mountains where red moons keep
cracking glaciers and calling her farther north.

Forty quick years   since I reached
into this river milk   for green boulders
grinding under glaciers   ducking heavy wings
of hemlock and cedar   winding again
through fireweed   and thimbleberries
the same old raven   chopping through mist
and smoke of slash piles   reminding me
that forty years with luck   will grind into a handful
of sparkling silt   and berries.

Montana

Shadow tentacles
rose from the bottom
of the lake, pulled me over
still gripping my fishing pole,
the green line still unwinding.

Stepdad

I am slightly afraid with your hands
under my back and head keeping me
from going under the algae-stained water
of the lake feeling your chest hairs against my boy's body
the lake level rising and sinking a little blurry
the smell of your man's skin still with me
sixty years later stronger than the taste
of sluggish lake water still in my mouth
that I learned to swallow without you ever
becoming the father I could swim back to
reach and kick you said and I did.

Skiff

Green line cutting deep
into wobbling lake shadows,
mind hooking darkness.
Drifting wild hours as a boy,
black waves shined like death,
rolled and glistened like my first trout.

Plough

After a rough man showed me
how to rip open the earth, I needed
to breathe its blackness, drink down
the sparkling sweet and bitter juices,
new furrows warm as flesh,
dark body safe enough to love.

Mother

A blue butterfly
keeps coming to the window
beside your garden,
beats against this splintered glass
where you're still waiting for me.

Silt sloughs away from spruce roots and the rotten
sleeper logs of a trapper's shack as the river drops, leaving
an island of deadwood near the mouth of an eddy
where a god-fearing neighbour abandoned his tractor
and his family, while the river took his land.

Whatever your dream or dogma, high water or broken
axles will stall your homestead vision, big summer
snow melt soak your plans, as the glacial peaks
blur behind your broken iron and a cloud
of mosquitos. Try adding some lemon and honey.

The spruce cabin timbers snap and check like gunshots
as August burns over clearcut mountain ridges
and up the dark river. The coffee tastes of silt,
the bacon is tough as old harness. The kids
say, *Dad, why are you so angry?*

RENOVATION

First a few classics
were tugged from the wall, like bricks
from crumbling mortar.
Gilt spines once propped the roof,
now river mist fills the rooms.

ANNIVERSARY

You have turned
the locks
of thirty-five doors
let all the keys

fall in rusty leaves
behind you
along the river
let thirty-five doors

swing open and slide
off their hinges
from a hundred coloured walls
into the river

unnumbered empty rooms
with their cries and footsteps
washing cold and silent
in a current of moonlight

down the river you know
will turn again
to a still pool of forgiveness
in cottonwood shadow.

After the long thrust unwinds
all the rope in your torso, sucks your breath
to the root of your spine, your mind
rushes out the rivet holes of your body
into space, flying north over the coast range.

Gouged and ice-chiseled basalt, wrinkling
glaciers, serpentine flows of silt and ice,
grey rock, green pools, rivers carving coastal jaws
of the Pacific crust to brutal edges and winding darkness
six miles beneath the blank page in my lap.

Below the turbine roar a thousand cries
of migrating tundra swans, ice cloud, and deeper
the howl of boulders tumbling, snapping of willow
and dogwood, moose feeding in drifted snow,
echo of a loon, a man loading his gun.

Punky balsam smoking beside my boots,
green riffles rattling shore gravel,
my boat tied to a fresh beaver stump,
granite whale back mountain rising across the channel,
ice-cut craggy bulkhead against the first black knives
of arctic winds and darkness, while the world
already in flames of the bloodiest winter
smokes from furrows of rubble and black flesh,
ten thousand unimaginable sinking purple skies
beyond us and far beyond the raven's wake-up call.

I've done nothing to deserve this
island and open water, ice-carved walls
rumbling cascades, wild cranberry and aspen flame,
this small fire on the razor edge
of a raven's wing, cold mountains
without a name, glacier-chewed rock
ribs and flows as far as one's eye or one's hope
can reach. I've done nothing
or given anything for such privilege that lets me
tie my boat to a fresh beaver stump.

CHANNEL CAMP, AUGUST

From blue ice
sharp claws
mountains ground down
to bright stones
come these
dark ripples
and clear light
we keep drinking
long days
with sliding
glaciers.

Music of stones
under clear water
rinsing brain cells
of time and grammar
cold river calling
chinook and sockeye home
under limestone mountain
big wings brushing
spruce and cottonwood
old man still
waiting in fireweed and berries
for grizzly bear
to come up
the steep bank
swat his pen
remind him
all guests of the river
share one story
getting pressed
in sand and gravel
bars downstream
in the deep
and clearest
currents of the world.

IV

SHORT STORY

I tied up my horse
and built a fire in the rain
as the river rose.
Homesteads kept floating downstream,
fresh trout cooked on the last coals.

Walking the shifting ice
to nowhere, along random fissures
that map my roadless days
on the frozen lake, low cloud
a drum skin stretching across
wind-polished summits
echoing the boom and crack
of a great movement
underneath. How thick
is the world that supports
such quick breathing
toward no destination,
how long before the dark
island shore breaks free
and a green wave rises
to swallow my shadow?

HEY MARMOT

(letter to Wayne)

Northern digger, fur-grateful friend, curling
up in scree stones and bunchgrass
roots, call when you know
the grizzly has gone somewhere else
to claw out a meal from the spring
snow melt, crawl out and call as raven
starts chopping open light in swamp spruce
and the last ice fog drains down the mountain,
sing back when you can see
sun snagging caribou antlers
above the frozen lake and snow geese
pulling pink cloud above us, call when it feels safe
to yell to another whose nerves
have had enough of winter
numbness in old bones.

TIME

As the old clock springs   and spur gears tighten
around your wrist and spine   like the choker cable
cutting through bark and sap   the shallow river
slows and shines bronze   fall raven ruckus so loud
you can't guess the hour   or remember your name.

Wood Butcher's Grave

Laid down in sword ferns
hemlock, black duff and deer bones
stumps and cedar lace.
What he loved and hurt
keeps twisting through maple roots.

Thirst

What taproot wanders
sideways through duff and stones
before boring deep?
Spring rain nectar drugs the heart
before one can live alone.

Her Amazing Legs

Always keeping far
ahead on the mountain trail,
never looking back—
the stranger following her
knows a waterfall is near.

Stone under Current

Take one more fossil
carved with my teeth from the breath
we made together,
toss it far from shore, some light
still moves the river we found.

Sting

Even with Buddha
guiding the clay you're coiling
through joyful hours,
a scorpion sleeps inside
the folds of your fine robe.

Where Is It?

He forgot where his skiff was tied
in some willow hook of the river.
Until he finds it
he won't forget the taste of her.

Across the Channel

With this year's turning
among the islands, some friends
no longer answer.
Through obsidian water
a skiff slides, a line unwinds.

Mandela

Night exploding trees
this coldest human winter
without a fire.
What heart will keep you awake
through all that falls around us?

In Tight Grain

Deep in the old-growth
stump heart, a few blood knots burn
like rubies, old friends'
closeness still in the center
of this spiral dark and light.

That he would   pull them
down from her   slippery
porch steps   out of the sooty
urban light   let them burst
and startle   his throat
with the same   sweet jelly
and joy   she had given him
without promises   the dangling
ripeness   of one season only
that would   not return.

Far from the rose light and rattler skin
stretched across Nevada sage and playa
and the thermal-riding raptor
with a gut full of digger squirrel,
a plunge west into dense green river walls
and muddy esteros will confound a haymaker.

I hadn't oiled my boots enough. Leaving greasewood
hummocks and badger holes for mushroom bog
and skunk cabbage sloughs, one needs a snorkel
and pontoons. By morning blackberry vines have crawled
over my tractor, algae has fowled the fuel line
and distributor, all my good iron is becoming phantoms
of rust sinking behind cedar stumps and pillars of moss
in the river mist.
                        I'm not ready
to become a fungi farmer. How does one slash through
these carcasses of green meat hanging from burly maples?
A clammy hand is crawling in my shirt.

I always figured the current
ran stronger, he joked
with his poet friend, as they muscled
their craft against a breeze from the coast
that stalled or turned them sideways
like a deadhead while they pumped
their makeshift paddles into each green curve
with ribald rhymes and laughter
as afternoon kept stretching out
under the wings of two following buzzards,
big-winged custodians accustomed to the foolishness
of men and the guts of steelhead.

No one believed it was bear
meat in the pie we were eating
with fine wine an artist brought
and poured for us all on the virgin
redwood deck at the cliff edge
as whales blew south toward Baja
through some residual oil slick
until I (in a finely woven meditation shirt,
gift from a hypnotherapist)
had to confess the killing.

Canteen and binoculars, no extended
metaphor slung around your neck.

Stunned in the middle of our damp
trail, you catch the elusive song

the feather flash and dying flame
in hummock and coyote bush, and guide

me deeper into thicket and dark ripples
of the bay slackened out beneath us

with praise and names of wintering water birds—
scoters, teal, whistlers, bufflehead "spirit ducks"—

as morning glides over the marsh grass
and poetic conceit is impossible.

    *

Though I can almost see you
giving a windfall Rome Beauty

to the exiled T'ang poet's donkey,
or slipping your own startled poem

into the little silk bag
slung from his saddle

with a thousand leaves
of gratitude and melancholy.

    *

But if not here, tasting the salt
and pollen whirring in mist wings

and exhalations of daybreak, you would
be reaching to some neighbour or stranger

frail or anxious with pain, you would
be offering your hands, and guiding him

toward home, or praise, the steady flight song
you keep hearing, and keep giving.

Whatever I stuttered   tossing your ashes
and bits of bone   into the creek—first
and final stream   you lived by—
last ripples   winding under Bixby Bridge
to the coast foam   whatever I tried to say
got lost mid-air   in the arc of my hand

years of mud roads   near each other
muttering now to the silent   water over stones
whatever I meant   to mix with your dust
scrap of words   swallowed by creek mist
from the arc of my hand   friendship and death
wash us with creek stones   grind and burn us

back to mineral   this chalky powder
that stays   in the pores of my hand
grooves of my palm   where words begin and end
ash of those we've loved   my hands keep.

A marsh hawk is carving the hour
as I wander wetland ponds
among nesting migrants—
snow geese, wigeons, bluebills—
rippling dark mirrors
near the sandhill cranes' long
deliberate steps.
                        Parting tall reed grass
I ponder migration and monogamy
and the mated birds' perfect homelessness.
What cosmic promise and wisdom
burns in the diamond brain
beneath a crane's tiny crimson cap?
What loneliness encloses and stalls
men's lives, while fears build the walls
where we make our songs? What wing
keeps spelling devotion above the water?

He once heard wild songs
repeat themselves. Now he hears
them change in mid-flight.
So the joy of one more day
with you makes each song breath new.

SALMONIDAE

Boatman chopping into a dark
swelling, with what desire
are you making the water restless?

Green line taut, pulling
under against the unknown
depths of glacial darkness

your slow breath
touching a light breeze
over the great movement

of lake, as a dragonfly
hangs beside you, holding you
in the still

rippling spruce shadow
beneath cold mountain
faces of stone and ice.

*

Green mirror
rocking my boat,
green line cutting

deeper as dusk begins
glazing the surface
and my mind

almost forgets to ask
what the invisible
might give, might tug

and startle my crude
motive, as the lure
travels cold thermal

zones, and the snake
deep in my limbic is coiled
to strike.

                *

Green line running
out through the eyes
of the rod, and down

through a nerve
in my arm
like a fuse, taut

with a primitive patience,
chrome spoon with a hook
and a few ounces of lead.

Until hunger yanks
and lights the fuse
I indulge a poetic

innocence, deep breathing
without metaphor, the dark underneath
floating such privilege.

                *

My dream pulse
snaps when it bites, big trout
jerking the nerve winding

from my old brain, as I reel
against the invisible
lake soul tugging

the rod and mountains bending
with the yank and dive, torque
of trout muscle

against my will.
Until the pull weakens
and a twisting light

rises from the clearest darkness
writhing beneath my boat
and my black net.

*

After I kill
and gut another gift
of glacial blood—sleek

moon-dappled green
and blue body with a rose
blush of twilight in its belly—

a loose hook
snags and stings
my throat.

How can I compose
a prayer or song
of gratitude, or deny

my predator,
never having
known hunger?

Ice melt keeps grinding
coloured stones where a tired man
takes his longest drink.
With sweet and bitter berries
the trail home startles and shines.

"After Lu Yu" refers to the T'ang Dynasty poet who reportedly
  wrote about eleven thousand poems.
"Danny Digs It" is for Dan Giddings.
"Dodging Backwater" and "Canoe Interruptus" are for Joe Millar.
"Hey Marmot" is for Wayne Merry.
Orpingalik was an Inuit shaman, one of Knud Rasmussen's
  principal informants.
"Poetic Life" is taken from one of Robert Bly's informal orations
  in a room of young writers.
"Raven Wing, Raven Eye," "Her Amazing Legs," and
  "Companionship" are for Judith Currelly, painter, pilot,
  and partner. The epigraph is from *Braided Creek: A
  Conversation in Poetry* (Port Townsend, WA: Copper
  Canyon Press, 2003), a poetic dialogue between Ted
  Kooser and Jim Harrison.
"The Sweater" is for Crystal Taugher.
"Winter Walk with Doc" and "Doc Says" are for Mike Whitt.
"What Won't Release" was written after a memorial for
  Norman Godbe.

Epigraphs: W.S. Merwin, "The Last One," *The Lice* (New York:
  Atheneum, 1969). Tu Fu, "Banquet at the Tso Family Manor,"
  One Hundred Poems from the Chinese, trans. by Kenneth Rexroth
  (New Directions Publishing, 1971).

Principal geographies alluded to in the poems are the northern
  California coast (Big Sur and Mendocino), the Robson Valley,
  British Columbia, and the Atlin Lake area of northern BC.

ACKNOWLEDGEMENTS

Grateful acknowledgement is made to the following presses and publications in which some of these poems appeared:

Man Living on a Side Creek: And Other Poems
(New York University Press, 1994).
Iron Fever (Sandpoint, ID: Lost Horse Press, 2003).
Alaska Quarterly Review
American Poetry Review
Bloomsbury Review
Dragonfly Magazine
Estero
Floating Island
Grain Magazine
Horsetails
The Malahat Review
Mānoa: A Pacific Journal of International Writing
Marin Poetry Center Anthology
Midnight Lamp
National Poetry Competition Winners' Anthology
Poetry Northwest
Prairie Fire
Puerto del Sol
Sonoma Mandala
Southern Poetry Review
Transfer Magazine
Willow Springs Magazine
Zyzzyva

Stephan Torre is the author of two previous collections, *Man Living on a Side Creek* (NYU Press, 1994) and *Iron Fever* (Lost Horse Press, 2003). His formative years were spent in western Montana, the northern California coast, and British Columbia. Though he's lived largely off-grid and in rural locations, his diverse working life includes college teaching, counselling and family services, farming, logging, and construction. Stephan lives in British Columbia.

ᐅᓈᐅ

OSKANA POETRY & POETICS
BOOK SERIES

Publishing new and established authors, Oskana Poetry
& Poetics offers both contemporary poetry at its best
and probing discussions of poetry's cultural role.

Randy Lundy—*Series Editor*

Advisory Board

| Robert Bringhurst | Louise Bernice Halfe | Duane Niatum |
| Laurie D. Graham | Tim Lilburn | Gary Snyder |

For more information about publishing in the series, please see:
www.uofrpress.ca/poetry